We are all alike. We often wonder "Why am I here?" and "Where am I going; what's the purpose of it all?" In 1975 I developed a plan to find answers to these questions. After several years of constant thorough and intensive study, I found the answers. Now I know what I believe and why I believe it. Previously I knew what I believed but didn't know why I believed it. I had my own homemade philosophy.

The root of my discovery was finding the Bible to be true. Its content is irrefutable as the Word of God as written in the original manuscripts. Virtually every religion was studied, tested and found to be either philosophical, full of contradiction or not provable. The Bible does not contradict itself in any way and its authenticity is well documented and provable.

God of the Bible answers why we are here by telling us that He wants to love and be loved; to fellowship with His created beings for eternity. Where I am going (after death) is also answered. We go either to Heaven or Hell. God wants us to follow His plan of instruction, trusting in Him. His salvation message is well documented in this handbook, condensed from His Word, the Holy Bible.

Some become angry about God's plan, raising their fist heavenward charging, "That's not fair! I didn't ask to be here!" That's correct, but it changes nothing. You are here. So, why not follow His simple instruction? God tells us that if we are too stubborn to listen to His plan, we will pay the consequences. Let us take a good look at His message with an open mind and heart.

--Jim Brown

ETERNITY
TOGETHER
You and I

A Handbook
of Biblical
Salvation Doctrine

By JIM BROWN, DBA

Scripture quotations are taken from Williams New Testament (WNT) or the New International Version (NIV) of the Bible for ease of understanding. **Boldface** and *Italics* typefaces and comments [inside brackets] are the author's privilege for emphasis and better understanding.

For additional copies write:

Jim Brown
2 Purnell Way
Palm Coast, Florida 32037

DEDICATION

Dedicated to Virginia D. Brown, my beloved mother, who lovingly displayed righteous living all of her life, always sacrificing herself for others. To my dear children, Steve, Pam, Lori and Carolyn, in fulfillment of my responsibility to God that they be given the truth of God's salvation message. Also to Dr. Walter R. Martin, my teacher, spiritual mentor and dear friend.

ACKNOWLEDGEMENTS

The author wishes to thank his wife, Anne Louise, for her tireless efforts in typing, editing and proofreading this manuscript. She is a blessing from God. Also daughter, Lori, and stepdaughter, Cherie, whose suggestions helped to keep this handbook simple and in the language of the people.

CONTENTS

INTRODUCTION

This handbook was given to you by someone who cares for you with tender affection and kindness. It is our desire to share with you how to find eternal life through God's message of salvation for all mankind; *His free gift for those who follow His instruction.*

Many who have been attending churches for years are unsaved simply because they have not been listening or the church has failed to thoroughly explain God's plan.

Many are not exposed to the message because they are not regular in church attendance or do not attend church at all.

Many have witnessed Christians or so called "professing Christians" in some form of misbehavior and have concluded that Christianity is not for them and thus refuse the message.

Many believe that God and His angels feed all of their good and bad deeds into a master computer and as long as the good outweighs the bad, they will be heaven bound.

Many believe that "God is love" and therefore, "Hell does not exist except for a few really bad people." Some refuse to acknowledge that a Sovereign Supreme God exists. Some believe they are a better person than most and place the ball in God's court to get them to heaven. Some believe that hell is on earth; that there is no heaven or hell after death.

Whatever category you are in is unimportant in itself. The important point is that you are given the truth of God's message of salvation so that you can accept or reject His plan. The decision is yours. It is your soul and your decision to make and no one else can make it for you. Your friend who gives you this handbook wishes only to give you this opportunity.

We are told by God:

"Go in by the *narrow* gate; for broad and roomy is the road that leads to destruction [Hell], and many are going in by it. But *narrow* is the gate and hard is the road that leads to life [Eternal], and few are they that find it." (Matthew 7:13,14; WNT)

What makes this road of salvation so narrow and hard to find? Mainly because God's plan runs counter to man's natural inclinations. Man has his own ideas as to how God will receive his soul in paradise; we do not listen to what God tells us. Which is more important: what we think or what God says? What we think is of no consequence at all.

It has been asked of me on numerous occasions, "What does God want from me?" After studying His Word, the Bible, the answer is simple. He wants us to trust Him; have faith and belief in what He tells us. That's all He asks from us. Such a request would not seem unreasonable from an Almighty, Sovereign

Supreme God who has created all things.

God gives us a clue when He writes:

> "For the message of the cross [salvation] is
> *nonsense* to those who are in the process of
> being *destroyed* [Hell], but it is the power of
> God to those who are in the process of being
> saved. For the Scripture says:
>
> 'I will destroy the wisdom of the wise,
>
> And I will set aside the learning of the
> learned.'" (I Corinthians 1:18,19; WNT)

God's message of salvation is simple--so simple
many choose not to believe in what He says. Some
pastors/teachers/evangelists oversimplify the message
by a quick recital of a confession of faith. Many
complicate the message by attaching much in the way of
legalism (*do's and don'ts*) to His plan. Neither should be
done. This booklet was designed to be more explanatory
than a pamphlet and less than a scholarly essay. That,
briefly but thoroughly, we may explain in "the language
of the people" God's one condition to receive His
otherwise free unmerited gift of salvation.

God's free gift of salvation is referred to as the
"*good news*" in some circles; the "*gospel*" in others. The
phrase "*born again*" is used to describe our salvation
condition from God.

Let us try, in the ensuing pages, to describe God's
plan; the substitutional sacrifice of Christ on the cross;
the deity [Godhood] of Christ; God's grace or our works
and deeds; heartfelt repentant attitude; human sin

versus God's Holiness; our confession of faith and false teachings. All of which are vital and part and parcel to understanding and fulfilling God's one condition of salvation for all mankind.

The greatest blessing we will ever receive is that of our eternal salvation and the internal everlasting peace that it gives to all that accept His free gift. That God may open your eyes and ears to the truth and understanding of His Word is the prayer that accompanies the gift of this handbook.

Jim Brown
Palm Coast, FL
July 1988

Chapter I

GOD'S PLAN FOR MAN
THE SUBSTITUTIONAL SACRIFICE
THE PLAN FOR OUR SALVATION

To fully understand the "substitutional sacrifice" of Jesus Christ on the cross, we should turn the clock back some two thousand years. For years I had heard this phrase without comprehending its importance. The custom of substitutionally sacrificing oneself is rarely practiced today; therefore, the phrase is somewhat meaningless to us. Many years ago it was commonplace for one man to pay another man's debts and thus prevent bankruptcy. The merchant didn't care who paid the outstanding balance on the debt as long as it was paid. A true substitutional sacrifice. How often does this happen today?

Another example of this custom was for a group of people to alternate serving a prison sentence for someone. Pretend for the moment that you were caught stealing food to feed your family. The sentence was six months in jail, the price one had to pay for such a crime. The judge or court system handing down such punishment did not care who paid the price for the crime as long as justice was served. A relative, neighbor or friend could substitutionally sacrifice a portion of their time to relieve you from jail so that you could provide for your family. This custom is no longer practiced today.

In like manner, God the Son provided the same type of substitutional sacrifice by dying on the cross as payment of punishment for our sins. Let's take a step back and see why this was necessary.

God tells us about His law:

    a. *Every* person over the age of reason or accountability has sinned and is judged guilty [see b. below] with the exception of the person of Jesus Christ. (Rom. 3:23)

    b. His *judgment and law* for this sin is the spiritual death of our soul or eternal condemnation [Hell} after our physical death. "The wages of sin is [spiritual] death." (Rom 6:23)

    c. God plays no favorites; all are treated alike regardless of the degree of sin - sin is sin - and all souls will be sentenced to eternal condemnation. (Rom. 3:22) [Yes, there are degrees of hell but that is another subject and of little consolation to us now.]

    d. His *justice* must prevail over His grace [unmerited favor], love and mercy [pity]--the price for sin must be paid--no exceptions. (Rom. 3:26)

Our Great and Almighty God has devised a manner by which all mankind can avoid His justice--God is a God of Justice, Love, Grace, Mercy and Truth. But God will not let His grace, love and mercy interfere with His justice--He says so. Therefore, our sins cannot be forgiven until the price or penalty is paid in full. Only then can God's justice be satisfied. Who other than God Himself could substitutionally sacrifice for you and me? No one, because we were condemned as sinners after committing our first sin. One sinner who is already sentenced cannot very well substitute for another sinner. So God Himself had to pay the price for our sins--for only

God is absolute perfection, without sin. Let us take a minute to read, in part, what God has to say about His plan for our salvation in Romans 3:21-26:

"But now God's way of giving men right standing [union] with Himself has come to light; a way without connection with the law, and yet a way to which the law and the prophets testify. God's own way of giving men right standing with Himself is through *faith in Jesus Christ.* It is for everybody who has faith, for no distinction at all is made. For everybody has sinned and everybody continues to come short of God's glory [perfection], but anybody may have right standing with God as a free gift of His undeserved favor, through the ransom [salvation] provided in Christ Jesus. For God once publicly offered Him in His death as a sacrifice of reconciliation [pardon] through faith, to demonstrate His own justice [for in His forbearance God had passed over men's former sins]; yes, to demonstrate His justice at the present time, to prove that He is right Himself, and that He considers right [not guilty] with Himself the man who has faith in Jesus." (WNT)

There is but one string attached to His condition for the forgiveness of our sins so that we may receive His free gift of salvation and spend eternity with Him.

The one condition is that we trust in what He has told us. *That through our heartfelt faith and belief, we recognize and accept His [Christ's] substitutional sacrifice for the forgiveness of our sins.* God is concerned only with our heartfelt belief, not just by what we think or say automatically. He knows man to be phony in this way: that we often say, do and think things that do not come from the heart.

God wants us in our hearts to realize that God the Son suffered on the cross for each of us--absorbing into His body the sins of all mankind from A to Z; from the beginning to the to the end of this age. We understand *why* He did it and *that* He did it, but we must trust Him as to *how* He did it. God says that if we make this confession with our mouth or lips and it comes from the heart, we are saved by His grace [undeserved favor] and mercy [pity], He has given us unmerited favor. The *how* of it all is explained by His having credited our account with righteousness and making us acceptable in His presence and sight. Without this bookkeeping entry, our souls would have been eternally condemned [hell].

The plan is simple and easy to understand. It is up to each individual over the age of reason to accept or reject His plan and instructions. If we reject the plan, God says we condemn ourselves and He takes no pleasure in rejecting anyone. Of one thing we may be certain--God will do everything He says He will without partiality to anyone. Many have conned and bluffed their way through life. Man sees only the external and is easily fooled, but we should be warned that God will not be conned for He knows our hearts.

To further confirm what has been written here, we need only to read the historical record of Christ's last words just prior to His physical death on the cross--*"It is finished!"* (John 19:30), meaning that He had "paid in full" the price for our sins. Through this payment, Christ literally purchased the souls of those who follow God's plan and who confess their faith and belief in His substitutional sacrifice. You and I then become Christ's property and a member of God's immediate family, heirs of the Kingdom of God and a permanent resident with God eternally [for ever and ever].

God has assured us through His Word, the Bible, that nothing is more important to Him than our eternal life [salvation] with Him. It is His desire that all of mankind be eternally saved and that no one be eternally condemned [hell]. He makes it clear, however, that only these two alternatives exist; there is no in-between. There is no purgatory as believed by some. There is no unconscious annihilation or suspended animation. There is no temporary residence for our soul in hell, later to graduate to paradise with God. Likewise, once credited with righteousness in God's sight, our residence is permanent in His Kingdom. Our souls never die nor sleep but instead find a home in either heaven or hell. Furthermore, it is our choice to make--not His. God makes it clear that if, through our heart we sincerely seek Him or knock on His door, He will indeed respond to our need for eternal salvation. Nothing, but nothing, would please Him more.

We are warned that only God knows the year, day and hour of our death. Thus it only makes logical sense that if we sincerely wish to have eternal life with God after our physical death, we should respond now. Based on the consequences, it does not make sense to roll dice with something as vital and important as our eternal salvation. Would you not agree?

This author does not operate under any illusions that all who read this will immediately fall to their knees and pray the confession of faith found in Chapter VI of this handbook. Nor does he believe in pressure or strong language to force the reader into conviction. To be convicted is between you and God and no one else. You are probably above average in intelligence; you know the difference between good and evil; you desire eternal life in heaven as opposed to hell as much as anyone. So when you are convicted by God in your heart, you will react. This information and instruction is only to help you react properly.

As a layman, I have studied virtually every religion known to man. All I can assure you is that every word you have read here is true and reveals to you the *only way* to receive salvation for your soul. As a teacher of God's Word, I know the penalty for distorting His truth and, rest assured, I do not wish to face His wrath. Nothing is worse than facing the wrath of Almighty God.

Now many people resent the fact or refuse to believe that there is only *one way* to receive salvation. They consider this fact to be quite narrow on God's part and thus unbelievable. Let us remember that it is an historical fact that Jesus Christ died on a cross through an act known as crucifixion. He declared Himself to be God-Man--Sovereign Supreme Deity--fully equal in nature to God the Father. History records these truths; not just Christian historians but secular (non-Christian) historians as well. Now it follows that Christ was either who He said He was or He was a liar. Even secular historians deny this assertion, claiming Him to be one of the most honest and truthful men who ever lived.

Simple logic follows: Would God in human flesh suffer the agony of crucifixion if there were multiple plans for the salvation of man? Why would God not simply offer other plans and thereby eliminate His own suffering? How could other plans pay for our sins and satisfy God's law of Justice, "...the wages of sin is [spiritual] death?" No other method is possible. If it were, we could be sure God would have offered it thereby making unnecessary His suffering on the cross. Be very careful when considering alternate plans unless, of course, you have found a self resurrection kit! Even then, I would personally prefer eternity with God Almighty.

To make your confession of faith complete, I must tell you of four qualifying issues that work hand in hand along with your knowledge of the substitutional sacrifice. Many of our TV evangelists and some pastors and teachers neglect these qualifications, not necessarily on purpose but often because of time limitations. These qualifying conditions are vital and important to the effectiveness and validity of your heartfelt confession of faith and thus need to be made a part of that confession:

Chapters:

Chapter II

THE DEITY OF JESUS CHRIST
GOD THE SON
THE WORD
AND THE TRINITY

It has been suprising to me, to discover by visiting many churches throughout this country, that there are a great number of people attending church regularly who do not know that Jesus Christ is God. Not only is He God, but fully equal to God the Father and the Holy Spirit. Jesus Christ's name before He became flesh was "The Word."

We are told by God the Holy Spirit through the apostle John, that in the beginning the Word [Jesus Christ] existed--the Word [Jesus Christ] was God Himself. It was through Him [Jesus Christ] that everything came into existence and apart from Him [Jesus Christ] not a single thing came into existence. It was by Him [Jesus Christ] that life began to exist. John 1:1-4

In order that our confession of faith be valid [acceptable], we must believe in our heart that Jesus Christ is God the Son. When the Word [Jesus Christ] manifested Himself in human flesh, He took upon Himself the identity of Jesus Christ and was thus called the Son of God. As the Son of God, He was fully *God-Man*--having His Godhood temporarily set aside to live as Jesus Christ in human flesh. He lived a perfect life and became the substitutional sacrifice for all mankind. Had He not set aside His deity to live in human flesh, He could not have become a sacrifice for us. Remember, to satisfy God's justice, He [Jesus Christ] had to be of human flesh living as you and I live but in absolute perfection.

Why is it so important that we have a heartfelt faith and belief in Jesus Christ as God the Son? Because God said so! Jesus Christ, Himself, tells us,

"I told you that you would die in your sins [Hell]; if you do not believe that I am the one I claim to *be* [God], you will indeed die in your sins." (John 8:24; NIV)

To die in your sins or "...the wages of sin is [spiritual] death" (Rom. 6:23) does not mean, biblically, that at our physical death our soul or spirit dies. It means a spiritual separation from God for eternity by going to hell. Remember our soul never dies.

Many of us have heard it said that Jesus Christ is our Lord and Saviour. Is it enough just to say that? Yes, *providing* that in our heart we understand the word "Lord" to mean God. If we believe that "Lord" is other than Sovereign Supreme Deity equal to God the Father, we would have difficulty with the validity of our confession of faith. It is frightening to further read what Christ has said,

"*Not everyone* who says to Me 'Lord, Lord' will get into the kingdom of heaven..." (Matt. 7:21)

Knowing Him simply as a "Lord" is not enough!

TRINITY

God tells us that the Father, Son and Holy Spirit is a *composite unity* of three separate personalities and is the One God. He tells us that all three persons have identical natures or attributes and are fully equal in power and authority. God further reveals that His major attributes are: 1) all knowing; 2) all powerful; 3) present everywhere at the same time. As Almighty God, His wisdom and powers are so far reaching and complex that our finite [limited] minds simply cannot comprehend. God does not insist that we understand how three personalities are One God, He only insists that we trust and believe in what He says. That is why Christianity is a faith--we must have trust and faith in what God tells us. Cult religions are just that--religions--because they are based on man's logic and interpretation as man would plan our salvation if he were God. Stay clear of them; exercise great caution if their plan for salvation differs from what you read in the Bible. (Chapter VII gives more detail.)

Do not get hung up on trying to understand how God accomplishes this trinitarian mystery. If He wanted us to thoroughly understand, He would have told us. "Water, for example, under pressure and in a vacuum at a given temperature below freezing exists simultaneously as both liquid, gas, and ice; yet it is identifiable always as water (H_2O), its basic nature. If our Creator can design a 'triple point of water,' He can surely be a triune God Himself..." (*Essential Christianity*, page 32)

Our finite [limited] mind immediately places the Son of God in a subordinate [secondary] position to the Father. We must not let this happen; for if we do, we can lose our soul for eternity. With God, when we create an organizational chart, we must look at the Father, Son and Holy Spirit as being on the same level. We should think in our mind, when the word God is mentioned, that we are talking about three personalities [separate individuals] as One in composite unity, fully equal to each other.

Christ was true deity and perfect humanity from birth to resurrection. We can believe in nothing less than a divine/human Redeemer, for God tells of none other than Jesus Christ. He lives today as God the Word and our Saviour. Salvation is possible only through Him. He states very clearly that, should we deny Him, He will deny us on judgment day. Should this happen, our souls would be eternally condemned.

Much more has been written and can be said on the deity of Christ and the Trinity doctrine. The purpose here is not to detail the nature of these truths but only to point out the need and necessity for trusting in these truths.

For those who request a more in-depth understanding of these topics, may we suggest the book, *Essential Christianity* by Dr. Walter R. Martin, published by Regal Books. This paperback can be purchased at your local Christian bookstore at a cost of $5.95 or less. Dr. Martin is the Founder and Director of the Christian Research Institute, a non-denominational and non-profit organization and regarded most highly by Christian scholars.

Chapter III

GOD'S GRACE
OR OUR WORKS AND DEEDS?
(SALVATION A FREE GIFT)

It is important for us to understand that our salvation as proposed by God's plan for man is a *free gift*; that we receive this free gift from God immediately following our heartfelt confession of faith in Jesus Christ. *The Good News is that salvation is free from God and that no amount of good works or deeds on our part contributes one iota to our salvation.*

God's grace is defined as His *unmerited or undeserved favor.* Such favor is given by Him in exchange for our heartfelt faith and belief in Jesus Christ and His substitutional sacrifice. When we are employed, we charge for the work that we do. Whatever wages we are paid we have earned because of our talent and ability. It can be said that we are entitled to our wages in exchange for our works and deeds.

But it is by God's grace that we have salvation -He has given to us, *who accept His gift*, His unmerited favor. To accept His gift is to make a verbal confession of faith as exampled in Chapter VI. God expresses it this way:

"For it is by My [God's] unmerited favor through faith that you have been saved; it is not by anything that you have done, it is My gift to you. It is not the result of what anyone can do, so that no one can boast of it." (Eph. 2:8,9; NIV)

God says we cannot earn our salvation or work our

way to heaven. God owes us nothing, for we have earned nothing. We are all sinners and the wages for our sin is eternal spiritual separation from God - an intellectual way of saying that without God's unmerited favor, we are all destined to hell.

Regardless of prior sins, anyone can receive salvation by following His simple instruction as outlined in the Bible (which is summarized in this booklet). *The qualifying issue here is to be sure that when making the confession of faith we realize from the bottom of our heart that salvation is a free gift from God and that we have done nothing to earn it.* Jesus Christ took upon Himself all of our sins, not part of them; sins committed past, present and future. In other words, salvation is a free gift resulting from God's substitutional sacrifice. It is not our good works plus Jesus Christ and His sacrifice. Salvation is only through faith and belief in Jesus Christ. When it comes to our salvation, our good works and deeds count as much as "...*filthy rags in His sight.*" (Isa. 64:6) They count for nothing at all--zero!

To me, this is Good News. But surprisingly, many people have a hard time accepting this portion of God's plan. Man has spent much of his time trying to be good enough to earn his salvation and accepting this simple concept is difficult. Man's finite [limited] mind, his ego and pride tell him he has to earn his place in heaven. Most of us think we are better than the average person and thus God owes us a seat in His kingdom. Many will tell you with their mouth that they think they are going to heaven when their heart is not at all certain. It makes them feel better to say it even though they are *truly* in doubt.

Those resisting God's instruction will immediately

respond in some fashion, asking, "Do you mean to tell me that a bad person can make a 'confession of faith' in Christ and then continue his sinful ways and be able to go to heaven?" No, that is not what God is telling us! We will learn in the next chapter that one of His qualifications to a valid [acceptable] "confession of faith" is a sincere heart felt repentant attitude. We have learned that God knows our heart and if a repentant attitude is not present at the time of our confession of faith, the commitment to God is not acceptable. Man cannot fool God. Aside from this important fact, there is another condition to consider when it comes to continuing sinful practice after our confession of faith.

We are told by God that if our desire for eternal life with Him is sincere and we accept His free gift, we will respond to Him in a loving manner with gratitude and appreciation. Our whole attitude toward God changes. A general feeling of loving kindness, goodwill and favorable regard for Him overwhelms our soul. This feeling produces a spiritual peace and joy and pleasure that is indescribable. Receiving God's unmerited favor brings about a deep seated feeling of gratitude and thankfulness to Him. Because of all these blessings, we want to please Him by living a more righteous life. It is not that we *have* to be a better person, it is that we *want* to be a more godly person. Human nature makes us hate to do what we feel forced to do but makes us happy to do what we want to do. That is why this new experience is called *born again.* We become a new person--a better person. Slowly and gradually this metamorphosis [change] takes place through growth in love for Him.

Quite naturally, the more we have sinned before our confession of faith, the greater the change--and often this produces a greater feeling of appreciation and gratitude. Those who have led a fairly righteous life may experience a lessor degree of change and therefore may not seem as grateful; but, nevertheless, the gratitude is there. We are all sinners wondering why we are here and where we are going when we die. Once the heartfelt confession of faith is made, this burden is lifted from our mind and heart.

What you have read is true. When you understand this process you can see why one could not make a genuine confession of faith and then continue to deliberately *practice* sinful ways. The key word is *practice*. We all continue to sin after we are saved; having salvation does not offer us perfection. We are still sinners but saved by His unmerited favor. We must enter into our new relationship with God with full intention to clean up our act. *We do not practice the same sin over and over again.*

PERSONAL TESTIMONY

Having had the *"born again"* experience, I can relate completely to God's definition of His grace. It was, indeed, a pleasurable experience delighting my soul and bringing about a new closeness to God. I found a love beyond any feeling that I had ever known; a loving kindness and goodness bursting forth toward God and my fellow man. While I knew I wasn't special, I felt special after having received His favor. A certain joy and peace came upon my heart that felt as though it was overflowing my soul. I can remember seeing and appreciating for the first time the beauty of His handiwork in His nature surrounding me. An overwhelming feeling of gratitude and appreciation to Him for my salvation seemed to flow through my body. A burning desire to help others share my experience was burdening my heart.

Yes, while I didn't realize it at the time, I was slowly becoming a new person as though I were "born again." To these things I can attest, offering my personal testimony. However, a word of caution is necessary here. I have related my personal experience but many born again believers with whom I have talked have had experiences less dramatic than mine. Many have had experiences more dramatic than mine. I have never found any two experiences to be the same. God knows the individual need for each of us that will confirm our salvation and instill the required appreciation for His love and grace. So, we should not compare our experiences. The point is that all must be born again to enter the Kingdom of God for He has made it clear,

"I tell you the truth, no one can see the kingdom of God unless he is *born again*." (John 3:3; NIV)

Did this experience cause me to live a perfect life without sin? No, not at all. I am still a sinner but now saved by His unmerited favor. While I continue to sin, I do not practice sinning the same sin over and over again because of my love and appreciation for God. When sinning I now become very conscious of it and immediately ask His forgiveness in Jesus' name and it is forgiven and forgotten as though it had never happened. See Chapter V.

Jesus Christ, our God and Saviour, paid the price for our sins serving God's justice through His sacrifice on the cross. The innocent [Jesus Christ] substitutionally sacrificed Himself for the guilty. God's mercy is His outward manifestation of *pity* given as a free gift by His grace or unmerited favor. The gift remains on the table for all to receive. Please do not reject His free gift of salvation.

Chapter IV

HEARTFELT REPENTANT ATTITUDE

We have discussed the substitutional sacrifice, the Sovereign Supreme Deity of our Saviour Jesus Christ plus the fact that it is not previous good works or deeds that contribute to our salvation but, rather, by God's unmerited favor alone we are saved. *Now we explain the necessity for man to have a heartfelt repentant attitude when making the confession of faith.*

We are informed by God that all of us are born knowing right from wrong. By instinct, our conscience tells us when we have committed an unrighteous act. Such unrighteousness can be as a result of our physical actions, what we say with our mouth or by what we think or imagine.

Let us take a look at the Biblical definition of the word "repent" or "repentance" - to change one's mind or purpose. Biblically speaking, repentance always involves a change for the better and chiefly has reference to repentance from sin. This change of mind involves both a turning *from* sin and a turning to God.

Christ began His ministry with a call to repentance by all individuals.

"Repent! for the Kingdom of heaven is near." (Matt. 4:17; WNT)

John the Baptist primed the pump for Christ's

message of the Good News by preparing the people to turn from sin toward God. In other words, to warn them to stop unrighteous acts and to practice righteous living.

"John the Baptizer appeared in the desert and was preaching a baptism conditioned on repentance to obtain the forgiveness of sins." (Mark 1:4; WNT)

God continually reminds us of the elementary teachings of repentance by laying the foundation that we cannot come to Him with a confession of faith without a willingness to discontinue practicing specific sins. Again, the key word here is *"practice"*. God knows that we are sinners; that we have sinned yesterday, today and will sin tomorrow. Just because we confess our faith and belief in Jesus Christ and His sacrifice for our sins does not mean that we will not sin any longer. Quite the contrary. God knows us all too well; that we are sinners until the day we die. God is telling us to take inventory of ourselves; if we routinely and continually *practice* a specific unrighteous act, we must discontinue that *practice*. We must have a heartfelt repentant attitude to discontinue such practice prior to making our confession of faith. God wants us to come to Him with a genuine intent to change our behaviour pattern or unrighteous lifestyle.

To some, this means a drastic overhaul of one's behaviour. To others, only moderate or minor alterations. Whatever our category, God wants us conditioned to accept change through our newfound experience. God promises to help us become a *new born again person*. Immediately following our heartfelt confession of faith the Holy Spirit enters our body and with His indwelling presence, our life automatically becomes more spiritual. He will assist us in resisting the temptations we are repenting of and will make us more aware of our sinful nature. For me, the Holy Spirit is the "bell ringer" within me. When I do, say or think something that is contrary to the will of God, I hear about it through the presence of the Holy Spirit. I then ask forgiveness for such unrighteousness with the intent to repent and I am forgiven. There are many additional blessings given to the believer by God, the Holy Spirit, with His indwelling presence. To elaborate on these blessings is not the purpose of this booklet, other than to say that we have a real treat in store for us once we are *born again*.

Within our nature it can be said that we have flesh and soul. Our flesh, by its nature, is selfish in that we are known to do what pleases ourselves. Our soul is largely representative of our personality with only a corner of it utilized for our spiritual nature. Generally, as we mature from adolescence, our flesh and personality become more united by crowding out our spiritual nature. Thus our flesh and soul predominate over our spiritual nature and we become more sinful. Once we are *born again*, God, the Holy Spirit, fills this void by spiritually dwelling in the believer and increasing our spiritual nature. A gradual change begins to take place and our selfish flesh and soul are influenced more and more by God and our spiritual nature. We are in the process of repentance, turning away from unrighteousness and turning to God. This does not happen overnight but is a gradual development. Because of our free gift of salvation, we have increased love and appreciation for God and our soul is eager to please Him. Our personality changes and we are in a *born again* posture.

Before this process can be accomplished, we must have a heartfelt repentant attitude, a willingness to change. God will complete this change within us if we permit Him to do so. Repentance involves deliberate turning from sin to righteousness. After one is *born again*, God *always* grants forgiveness when there is genuine, heartfelt repentance.

If you look upon repentance meaning that you must be perfect before you make your confession of faith, you will never make the confession. So, erase that from your mind. If that were the case, you would feel that you were offered salvation by your works and deeds and that simply is not true. All God wants from you prior to your confession of faith is a *heartfelt repentant attitude.* Once you are saved, the Holy Spirit living within you will help you in resisting specific temptations of unrighteous living.

Here are a few words from God on repentance:

"For the sorrow that comes in accordance with the will of God results in *repentance* that leads to *salvation* and leaves no regrets;..." II Cor. 7:10

"...because He is really dealing patiently with you, because He is not willing for any to perish [Hell] but for all to have an opportunity to *repent*." II Peter 3:9 (WNT)

Chapter V

HUMAN SIN VS. GOD'S HOLINESS

When we discuss sin, we must discuss God's Holiness as well, for it is because of His Holiness that we are condemned by our sin. *The qualifying issue of this chapter is that while making our confession of faith, we must acknowledge to God the Father that we are a sinner.* It is surprising to learn how many people will deny that they have ever sinned. God makes His position clear on this subject:

"If we confess our sins, He is to be depended on, since He is just, to forgive us our sins and to cleanse us from every wrong. If we claim *'We have not sinned,'* we are making Him a liar and His message is *not* in our hearts." I John 1:9,10 (WNT)

Just what is sin as defined by God? To sin is to violate one or more of God's laws after we reach the age of reason or accountability. Sin can also be expressed as a transgression against God or our disobedience to His will. Sin can be manifested by what we say, or in some cases by what we do not say; in what we do as a physical act or deed; by what we think or imagine.

God informs us that all of mankind has sinned. Some sin is deliberate, while some is accidental. While God hates all sin, there are degrees of sin. The point is that in the eyes of God, sin is sin regardless of how it is manifested or whether it be major or minor. God has already predetermined the penalty for our transgressions; the payment for sin is spiritual separation from Him with a penalty of eternal condemnation [Hell]. No one can escape this judgment. The moment we commit our first sin, after the age of reason, we are spiritually condemned.

As we have learned, our sin condemns us. We must find a way to have these sins forgiven, otherwise a Holy God cannot accept our soul into His presence at all--let alone for eternity. God's plan provides this forgiveness through faith and belief in Jesus Christ and His substitutional sacrifice. God says there is no other way to heaven but through God the Son, Jesus Christ.

It is interesting to read what God says, through Paul, about the subject of sin and Jesus Christ:

"So I find this law: When I want to do right, the wrong is always in my way. For in accordance with my better inner nature I approve God's law, but I see another power operating in my lower nature in conflict with the power operated by my reason, which makes me a prisoner to the power of sin which is operating in my lower nature. Wretched man that I am! Who can save me from this deadly lower nature? Thank God! *it has been done through Jesus Christ our Lord*! So in my higher nature I am a slave to the law of God, but in my lower nature, to the law of sin." (Romans 7:21-25, WNT)

Through the Holiness of God's Law, the true nature of sin was designed to be manifested to our conscience. Sin is an organized power, acting through the members of the body. The seat of sin is in our will; we sin by our own freewill choice and can blame no one but ourselves for it. The more we sin the less our conscience reminds us and the less guilt we feel about our transgressions. Sin becomes habit.

If we rob a bank and are apprehended, we have committed a crime against society and we will have to pay the penalty for breaking the law. Likewise, when we sin against God we are immediately "caught in the act" because we cannot hide from Him; He knows all that we do, say or think. Because we have committed a crime against God we will have to pay the spiritual penalty for breaking His moral or spiritual law. God has given us the verdict beforehand so that we can avoid the punishment. Someday our soul will stand before God and we will be judged. When this time comes, there is only one attorney [figuratively speaking] to "hire"--Jesus Christ. However, God's law reminds us that we must engage His services before we experience physical death. To employ His services cost us only two minutes of our time. If, after reading this handbook, you feel eligible to meet the simple qualifications described herein, simply get on your knees and pray the "confession of faith" shown in Chapter VI. If we refuse to follow His simple instruction, He tells us that we have condemned ourselves. Salvation is ours for the asking providing we have heartfelt faith and belief in His plan--the only qualification to be eligible.

Not only must we have our past and present sins forgiven but our future sins as well, for we know that after we make our confession of faith we continue to sin. When Christ was on the cross, He absorbed into His body a lifetime of sin for all mankind. As a *born again* believer, my future sins are forgiven. Christ does it all!

Once the confession of faith is made and we are

born again we become a member of God's immediate family and heir to His throne. Thus, when we sin, we are disobedient to His will and subject to His discipline. To avoid His discipline, we must immediately ask forgiveness of that specific sin with the heartfelt intent to not *practice* that sin any longer. We are forgiven, praise God! If we do not ask forgiveness, we are still saved but living outside of His favor. All of this can be compared to raising children. When they are bad they must be disciplined but when they say they are sorry and promise not to do it again--you forgive them--the fellowship is immediately restored and all is forgiven and forgotten. So it is with God once we have made a confession of faith and have become a member of His family. How is this possible? Because Jesus Christ answers our prayers for forgiveness--we are owned by Him--He bought and paid for our soul on the cross. We are His property and He guarantees us forgiveness once we recognize our sin in this fashion.

God has given us the Ten Commandments as a guideline to show us when we step out of His moral boundaries. Through these, we are shown major areas of disobedience to His will. However, there are over 600 other sin areas mentioned in the Bible, so we need not remain smug with our self-righteousness if we tenaciously adhere to the Ten Commandments only.

The unsaved or unbeliever is not a member of God's immediate family. Their sins continue to pile up, one upon another until their physical death. Then Judgment Day. There is no forgiveness for them. Hell is not a very nice place and not a popular topic of conversation! It is, however, the only alternative for those who reject God's salvation message. The positive side of Hell is that no one has to go there. They only go there by stubborn refusal to listen to what God has said. The author is not saying this to scold but as a point of fact. It should be pointed out that Jesus Christ, during His ministry on earth, talked more of Hell than of Heaven. We have been warned and have no excuse. The question remains--do we care enough to find the truth? Many people spend more time buying a home or automobile than they spend searching for their means of salvation. In a nutshell, there is only *one unforgivable* sin--lack of faith and belief in Jesus Christ as God and Saviour of the world.

HOLINESS

We will close this final chapter on qualifications with a brief discussion about God's Holiness. We have said that "...it is because of His Holiness that we are condemned by our sin." What do we mean? God's Holy nature forbids Him to fellowship with a sinner. He simply cannot be in the presence of sin. We have said that God's purpose of creation is to mutually exchange love and fellowship with His created beings. An unforgiven sinner does not fulfill God's original purpose of His creation.

The only way a sinner can fulfill the intended purpose of God is to confess his faith and belief in Jesus Christ and His substitutional sacrifice along with the four qualifying issues as outlined. God has promised that once this is accomplished, He will credit our account making us righteous in His sight. A simple "bookkeeping entry" forgives us a lifetime of sin. Now, how He does it and why it works that way is not explained. We must have faith, belief and trust in what He tells us. To enact our salvation is most assuredly a leap in faith. For this faith our rewards are great--eternal life for our soul fellowshipping with God Almighty.

This same Holiness guarantees us a God that is absolute, perfect in all things. He means what He says and says what He means without partiality to anyone. For the *born again believer* He promises to forget our sins, casting them into the farthest depths of the sea. What a neat promise for those of us who have not behaved as we should.

God wants His created beings to care enough to search for Him--to find the truth of our salvation through His Word, the Bible--to trust Him--to humble ourselves before Him--to pray for the truth to be revealed to us. The truth of salvation will set us free.

Chapter VI

OUR CONFESSION OF FAITH

We have now completed God's salvation plan for man. We turn to God's Word, the Holy Bible, for our final instruction for it is "...the sacred Scriptures which can give you wisdom that leads to salvation through the faith that leans on Christ Jesus. All scripture is inspired [breathed on] by God..." (II Tim. 3:15:16)

God gives final instruction:

"But what does it say? 'God's message is close to you, on your very lips and in your heart'; that is, the message about faith which we preach. For if with your lips you acknowledge the fact that Jesus is Lord [God], and in your hearts you believe that God raised Him from the dead, you will be saved. For in their hearts people exercise the faith that leads to right standing, and *with their lips* they make the acknowledgment which means *salvation.* For the Scripture says, 'No one who puts his faith in Him will ever be put to shame.' But there is no distinction between Jew and Greek, for the same Lord is over them all, because He is infinitely kind to all who call upon Him. For everyone who calls upon the name of the Lord will be saved." (Romans 10:8-13; WNT)

To summarize what has been written thus far, we offer the following statements:

Essentially there is but one condition to receive

salvation. This condition requires, by God, a heartfelt faith and belief in the substitutional sacrifice of our God and Saviour [Jesus Christ] and in His resurrection. It is only reasonable to assume that, in order for some to believe from the heart, background information must be given for greater understanding of this sacrifice. We tried to do that.

There are four qualifying issues that accompany this one condition of salvation. These issues are assumed to be part and parcel of the one condition but are sometimes overlooked. These issues are detailed in this handbook for greater understanding. They are not here to complicate God's simple plan; only to assure the validity [acceptance] of our confession of faith. We summarize them here:

We must believe that Jesus Christ *is God* and fully equal in power and authority to God the Father.

We must believe that our salvation is a *free gift* from God and not because of any works or deeds that we have done.

We must, if we are *practicing* sin prior to the confession of faith, have a *repentant attitude* to turn from this sin--turning toward God and a more righteous lifestyle.

We must admit that we are a *sinner* and that we have sinned in the past and present with the full realization that we will sin in the future. Confessing our faith brings about salvation, not perfection.

These qualifying issues are simple to understand. They are not unbearable burdens that would prevent a person from accepting God's plan. The primary one condition of salvation is fully detailed in Chapter I. If you understand and accept the content of that chapter and subsequent chapters, you are *eligible* to confess your faith and belief in Jesus Christ and His sacrifice. With this instruction, we have a solid foundation upon which to pray the following prayer. We urge you to pray now, for only God knows our lifespan.

CONFESSION OF FAITH

Dear Heavenly Father,

I come to You admitting that I am a sinner. I believe that Jesus Christ is God the Son and that He died on the cross for the forgiveness of my sins. I know that my sins are forgiven by Your unmerited favor, not by my works or deeds. I repent of my sins and pray that You give to me eternal salvation as You have promised.

In Jesus' Name, I pray. Amen.

For those of you who have made your heartfelt confession of faith, **you are saved!** The Holy Spirit now dwells inside of you and will comfort and give you peace. As a child of God and a member of God's family, you need to fellowship with your brothers and sisters in Christ. May you be encouraged to find a local Bible teaching church. You need the food and enrichment of God's Word from a Bible study class. There is much to learn about God--His nature, and some of the blessings to be received now that you are *born again*. God also requests you to be baptized as an outward sign of your faith and as an example to encourage others to partake of God's free Gift. Your salvation can never be taken from you. May God bless and keep you and give you everlasting peace.

For those of you who did not make the confession of faith but are interested in gaining your salvation, I suggest that you reread this handbook. Also, may I encourage you to find a loving Bible oriented church where the pastor can help you with your decision. Perhaps you have questions not answered in this handbook that could be answered by a loving pastor. Whatever the reason for your indecision, please do not delay in seeking your salvation.

Above all, read Chapter VII so that you are aware of the authorized Bibles and can recognize those religions that are antichrist in their teachings. Cult religions are popping up all over the landscape. *Be certain that the church of your choice teaches the Trinity doctrine and that Jesus Christ is God.* May God open your eyes and ears so that you can discern the truth and may He bless you with His salvation. Amen.

Chapter VII

FALSE TEACHINGS

Most of us know what we believe but we simply do not know why we believe it. Perhaps it is time that we establish a sound basis for our belief. We all have a tendency to piece together our experiences over the years and conclude for ourselves a method by which God will bring our souls into an eternity of heavenly bliss. Over the past thirteen years, I have talked with hundreds of people on this subject. Most of them had a plan--their own. No two plans were ever the same. The only common denominator that I found was how they all began their explanation, i.e., "I *believe* God will or would...."

After listening for a few minutes I would ask them the following question, "Which, do you think, is most important? What you believe, think or say, or what God believes, thinks and says on the subject?" Without exception, all would respond, "God, of course!" The logical question follows: why not go to the source--God, Himself. God wrote sixty-six books on the subject using over forty authors without error, inconsistency or contradiction. These books were bound together to form a masterpiece called the "Bible". Within the confines of the Bible, God has taken great care to protect what He has written about His nature, attributes and His plan of salvation for you and me.

What you have read here comes from the Bible in summary form and relates the truth of what God has said about His salvation message for all mankind. There are over thirty versions of the Bible being printed today--each telling of the same plan, but worded differently. Publishing the Bible is big business--a multibillion dollar industry. In a free enterprise system you can well understand why so many versions are printed . Each publisher hopes that his particular rendering is better understood than the others and thus will obtain a larger percentage of the market share. Since the salvation message is not distorted, there is nothing wrong with many versions being printed. Here is a list of twenty nine versions which comprise a partial list of published Bibles accepted by the Christian community each giving the identical message of salvation:

The American Standard Version
The King James Version (Original and Revised)
The New International Version
Good News Bible
The Revised Standard Version
The New American Standard Bible
The New English Bible
The New Testament of Our Lord and Saviour Jesus Christ
The New Testament (Henry Alford)
The New Testament in Basic English
The New Testament in the Language of Today (Beck)
The Berkeley Version of the New Testament (Verkuyl)
The Epistles of Paul (Conybeare)
The New Testament: An American Translation (Goodspeed)
The New Testament in the Translation of Ronald Knox
The New Testament: A New Translation (Moffatt)
The Centenary Translation: The New Testament in Modern English (Montgomery)
The New Testament: A New Translation (Norlie)
The New Testament in Modern English (Phillips)

The Book of the Acts (Rieu)
The Four Gospels (Rieu)
The Emphasized New Testament: A New Translation (Rotherham)
The Living Bible (Taylor)
The Twentieth Century New Testament
The New Testament in Modern Speech (Weymouth)
The Williams New Testament
The Amplified New Testament
Young's Literal Translation of the Holy Bible
New Jerusalem Bible

Now this brings us to the subject of false teaching. We are warned over and over by God to avoid those who falsely teach His message. Many of these false teachers and religions contend to be Christian even using the name "Christian" and talking reverently about the Bible. Some use Christian terms and phrases that sound valid to the innocent but have entirely different meanings. Some use the Bible to win your confidence but once you are inside the church, the Bible is set aside in favor of the founder or leader's writings. Some may even pick and choose selected verses of scripture to make a point for their cause but never really study the authorized version of the Bible. Such is the deception of cult religions that teach contrary to God's salvation message. According to the Bible, their doctrines, if believed and followed, will indeed cost you your salvation and condemn your soul for eternity. God warns us accordingly:

II Peter 2:1-3 -- Now there were false prophets among the people, just as there will be false teachers among you too, who will insidiously introduce destructive heresies and deny the Master [Jesus Christ] who has bought them, thus bringing on themselves swift *destruction* [Hell]. Many people will follow their immoral [shameless] ways, and because of them the true Way will be abused. In their greed they will exploit you with messages manufactured by themselves. From of old their condemnation has not been idle and their destruction has not been slumbering. (WNT)

Acts 20:30 -- Even from your own number men will appear who will try, by speaking *perversions of truth*, to draw away the disciples after them. (WNT)

II Timothy 4:3,4 -- For a time will come when they will not listen to wholesome teaching, but to gratify their own evil desires will surround themselves with *teachers* who teach to gratify their own evil desires, because their ears are itching so to be tickled, and they will cease to listen to the truth and will turn to listen to myths. (WNT)

I John 2:22,23 -- Who is the *notorious* liar, if it is not the man who denies that Jesus is the Christ [God]? He is the real Antichrist, the man who disowns the Father and the Son. No one who disowns the Son can have the Father. Whoever owns the Son has the Father too. (WNT)

Following is a list of cult religions that should be avoided. This list is by no means complete. If you are in question as to the authenticity of any church group, contact Christian Research Institute, P. O. Box 500, San Juan Capistrano, CA 92675; phone: (714) 855-9926.

List Of Cult Religions:

Ascended Masters
Black Muslims
Christadelphianism
Christian Science
Church Universal & Triumphant
Discipleship & Submission Movement
EST - Werner Erhardt
Eckenkar
Edgar Casey & Reincarnation
Freemasonry
Hare Krishna
Hinduism
Holistic Health or Healing
Jehovah's Witnesses
Jesus Only Movement
Manifestations of the Sons of God
Meher Baba
Mormonism
New Age Movement Church
Nichiren Shosha Buddhism
Reorganized LDS Church
Reverand Ike
Scientology - Dianetics
Self Realization Fellowship
Silva Mind Control
Spiritism
The Children of God
The Mind Sciences
The Walk
The Way International
The Worldwide Church of God
    (Herbert W. Armstrong's Plain Truth Magazine)
Transcendental Meditation (TM)
Unification Church (Sun Myung Moon)

Unitarianism
Unity School of Christianity
William Branham
Yoga
Zen Buddhism

Having gone this far, there may be some who will honestly reflect a state of confusion not knowing who or what to believe. I can certainly relate to this confusion for I have been there myself. I can remember the day that I squared my jaw, got on my knees and prayed to God to lead me to the *truth* of His message. He did just that. Perhaps it is time for you to do the same thing. God promises to answer our plea providing our interest is sincerely heartfelt. Why second-guess His plan of salvation when we have an invitation to go to the Source of that plan?

For others, it is time to make your confession of faith. There is nothing miraculous about the words used in Chapter VI for there are many such written statements, one just as effective as another. The miracle is God's unmerited favor and pity, through God the Son Jesus Christ. God credits our account making us righteous in His sight and heir to His kingdom; giving us life everlasting with Him. Go to your knees in the privacy of your home and confess your faith from the heart. **You will be saved!**

May the Lord God bless you with His salvation so that we may spend *eternity together--you and I.*

Appendix:
Terms Defined

WORD AND PHRASE DEFINITIONS
AS THEY APPLY TO THE CONTENT OF THIS HANDBOOK

WORD AND PHRASE DEFINITIONS AS THEY APPLY TO THE CONTENT OF THIS HANDBOOK

ABSOLUTE -- God's condition of perfection in all things.

ACCOUNTABILITY -- the age of youth to reason for themselves and their election to sin.

ALMIGHTY -- All powerful

ANTICHRIST -- anyone who does not believe Jesus Christ to be God, the Second Person of the Trinity. (Second Person does not mean secondary position or title.)

BELIEVER -- one who is Born Again after the Confession of Faith.

BIBLE -- God's Word as written in the original manuscripts.

BORN AGAIN -- the new condition of a person after he has received salvation by God's unmerited favor through faith and has the Holy Spirit Living in him.

CHRISTIAN -- those who have made a confession of faith and are Born Again.

CONDEMNATION -- a condition of our soul resulting from unforgiven sin of the unsaved, sending our soul to Hell for eternity; opposite of salvation.

CONFESSION OF FAITH -- we must, with our lips, confess our heartfelt faith and belief in God's plan of salvation for all mankind. (See Chapter VI)

CULT RELIGIONS -- a group of people who gather to worship a form of man's concept of religion--great devotion to a person, idea or thing--considered unorthodox and in error to the truth of God's Word.

DEITY -- God

DESTROY/DESTRUCTION -- of the soul in Hell for eternity.

ETERNITY/ETERNAL -- forever and ever, with no end.

FAITH -- heartfelt belief in the unseen as told by God through the Bible.

FALSE TEACHERS -- people who teach doctrines contrary to God's Word, the Bible.

FINITE MIND -- a mind that is limited by its human inadequacies. God's wisdom is infinite.

FREE GIFT -- A gift from God that has not been earned by works or deeds. Example: salvation is a free gift of God's unmerited favor and made possible through our faith in Jesus Christ.

GOD -- perfect in power, wisdom, and goodness whom men worship as Creator and Ruler of the universe.

GOD-MAN -- God, Jesus Christ in human flesh.

GOOD NEWS -- God's free gift of salvation for all mankind.

GOSPEL -- God's salvation message from the Bible.

GRACE -- God's unmerited or underserved favor.

HEARTFELT -- faith and belief that comes from the heart as well as the head

HEAVEN -- a resting place for the souls of the saved with God for eternity.

HELL -- a place of torment for the souls of the unsaved for eternity--separation from God.

HOLINESS -- God's nature prohibiting His presence or fellowshipping with a sinner or sin.

JESUS CHRIST -- Sovereign Supreme Deity, God the Son, The Word, Son of God

JUDGMENT OF GOD -- God's justice condemning the unforgiven sinner and rewarding the believer for post Born Again deeds in His behalf.

JUSTICE OF GOD -- Wages of sin is spiritual death, eternal life in Hell for the unbeliever (unsaved). Rewards for the believer for his deeds in glorifying God after being Born Again.

LAW -- God's laws (over 600) as disclosed in the Bible.

LORD -- God

MANIFESTED -- to disclose through--to display.

MANKIND -- the human race.

MERCY -- God's pity. God has shown all mankind his pity through His salvation message (Christ's sacrifice). Provides for the salvation of those who die before the age of accountability.

MESSAGE OF GOD -- God's plan of salvation for His created beings.

ONE CONDITION -- God's one condition making all mankind elegible to receive His free gift of salvation, i.e. heartfelt faith and belief in Jesus Christ's sacrifice in payment for our sins.

PARADISE -- Heaven.

PHILOSOPHICAL -- man's theory not based on fact.

PLAN OF GOD -- His salvation message or instruction for all mankind.

PRACTICE -- to not continually or habitually practice a specific sin over and over again.

QUALIFYING ISSUES -- accompanying the one condition of salvation as outlined by God and defined in this handbook.

RELIGION -- based upon man's theory, not from God's Word, the Holy Bible.

REPENTANCE -- turning from sin toward God or a more godly lifestyle.

SALVATION -- a status in which God secures our souls with Him forever (i.e. no condemnation)

SAVED -- our state after confessing our faith in Jesus Christ as Saviour of all mankind, looking forward to an eternity with God in heaven.

SAVIOUR -- Jesus Christ, One and Only to save all of mankind.

SCRIPTURE -- God's Word as recorded in the Holy Bible from the original manuscripts.

SIN, SINNER -- a violation of God's law(s); disobedience to His will, a transgression against Him.

SOUL -- indwells the human body assigned to heaven or hell after physical death but never dies.

SOVEREIGN -- supreme power, absolute in all things, unlimited, exhalted, accountable to no one but Himself.

SPIRITUAL DEATH -- a separation from God. Our soul, after physical death, taking up residence in Hell for an eternity.

SPIRITUAL SEPARATION FROM GOD -- to the unsaved, eternal condemnation to Hell; to the saved, subject to God's discipline.

SUBSTITUTIONAL SACRIFICE -- Christ's death on the cross in payment for a lifetime of sin for all mankind.

THE WORD -- Jesus Christ, His preexistant heavenly Name.

TRANSGRESSION -- Sin.

TRINITY -- Father, Son and Holy Spirit, three separate personalities all with identical natures and attributes, are the One God. A composite unity of co-equality.

UNBELIEVER -- one in the state of rejecting God's plan of salvation.

VALID/VALIDITY -- acceptable, acceptance, making one eligible for salvation.

WAGES OF SIN IS DEATH -- spiritual expression relating to the condemnation of the unbeliever's soul in Hell.

WORD -- either biblical scripture or "The Word", the name for Jesus Christ as He sits at the right hand of the Father in heaven and His Name prior to having been born in human flesh.